IT WORKS!
Revolution in
Construction

Lynette Brent Sandvold

11/09

This edition first published in 2010 in the United States
of America by Marshall Cavendish Benchmark.

Marshall Cavendish Benchmark
99 White Plains Road
Tarrytown, NY 10591
www.marshallcavendish.us

All Internet addresses were available and accurate when this book went to press.

Library of Congress Cataloging-in-Publication Data

Sandvold, Lynette Brent.
Revolution in construction / by Lynette Brent Sandvold.
p. cm. -- (It works!)
Summary: "Discusses the history of construction, how the technology was developed,
and the science behind it"--Provided by publisher.
Includes bibliographical references and index.
ISBN 978-0-7614-4378-0
1. Building--History--Juvenile literature.
2. Engineering--History--Juvenile literature. I. Title.
TA149.S36 2010
624.09--dc22
2008054363

Cover: Q2AMedia Art Bank
Half Title: Shutterstock.
P7cl: Shutterstock; P7cr: Jon R Peters/Fotolia; P7bl: Karim Hesham/iStockphoto;
P7br: Dreamstime; P11cl: BlueMoonPics/iStockphoto; P11ct: Bettmann/Corbis;
P11cr: Henryk Sadura/shutterstock P11br: Shutterstock; P15: Shutterstock;
P15(inset): Shutterstock; P19cl: Photo Channel/Photolibrary;
P19cr: javarman/Shutterstock; P19bl: Quayside/Dreamstime; P19br: Corbis;
P22: Dreamstime; P22cr: Shutterstock; P22t: Corbis; P27: iStockphoto.
Illustrations: Q2AMedia Art Bank

Created by Q2AMedia
Series Editor: Jessica Cohn
Art Director: Sumit Charles
Client Service Manager: Santosh Vasudevan
Project Manager: Shekhar Kapur
Designer: Shilpi Sarkar
Illustrators: Aadil Ahmed, Rishi Bhardwaj,
Kusum Kala, Parwinder Singh and Sanyogita Lal
Photo research: Sakshi Saluja

Printed in Malaysia

135642

Contents

Giant Stones

The pyramids in Egypt are amazing. People look at them and wonder: *How did the Egyptians move those giant stones?*

It remains a mystery how the Egyptians moved the giant stones. We do know which pyramid was built first, though. It was a step pyramid made for King Djoser. Most of the covering around that pyramid is gone, so we can see how it was structured.

Above ground, there were six **mastabas** piled on top of one another. A mastaba is a flat-roofed building used as a tomb. The Egyptians made most mastabas of mud-brick or of wood. The mastabas of the step pyramid were made of stone. The step pyramid was the first major work in stone. It "paved the way" for other stone structures.

Meet Imhotep

Can you imagine working as a doctor *and* an **architect**? Imhotep did both those jobs. He was a priest and poet, too. He even found time to advise the king. Imhotep may be the most famous ancient Egyptian who was not a royal. Many people thought Imhotep was part of a legend. Then proof was found to show he was a real person. Researchers believe that Imhotep treated more than two hundred diseases during his lifetime. Some say Imhotep invented papyrus, which is a kind of paper made from a plant. Imhotep is best known, however, as an architect. He made the first stone monument.

I have to take time from my medical practice. The pharaoh wants me to design a building.

We will start with a large mastaba. Then we will put smaller mastabas on top.

The mastabas will form steps.

Being smart and talented helps in Egypt. I get to work with royalty!

5

Lift It Up!

12-inch (30½-centimeter) ruler

pencil with flat sides

40 or so pennies

table or other flat surface

 1 Place a pencil on a table. Place a ruler across it at the 4-inch (10-cm) mark. The pencil acts as a **fulcrum**. A fulcrum is the spot on which a **lever** rests when it is lifting something.

 2 Place ten pennies on the ruler within the 1-inch (2½-cm) mark. The pennies should be between the pencil and the "short" end of the ruler.

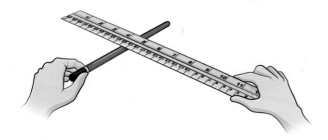

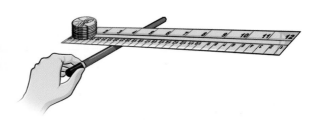

 3 Add pennies to the other end until the ten pennies are lifted. Record the number of pennies it took to lift the ten pennies.

 4 Remove the pennies. Move the pencil to the 8-inch (20-cm) mark. Repeat, placing the pennies on the "long end" of the ruler. You can see that the distance between the load and the fulcrum makes a difference.

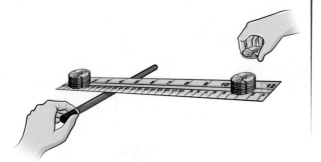

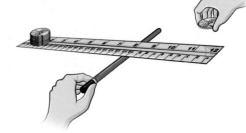

WHO WOULD HAVE THOUGHT?

Architectural Wonders

Ancient builders made astounding structures in Mexico and elsewhere. Modern **skyscrapers** are astounding, too, but the ancients made huge structures without modern **technology**. The Great Pyramid at Giza, for example, was the tallest building on Earth for nearly four thousand years. Centuries ago, the ancient Romans built **aqueducts** to carry water. These aqueducts could supply 35 cubic feet (1 cubic meter) of water per day per person. That's more water than most of us use each day. Then there is the Great Wall of China. The Great Wall is a series of walls and buildings made of stone and earth. It is well over 4,000 miles (6,437 kilometers) long. The wall is ancient, yet visitors can still walk on many of its sections.

pyramid in Chichen Itza, Mexico

Great Wall of China

pyramids at Giza, Egypt

aqueduct

Reaching for the Sky

The word *skyscraper* didn't exist until the 1880s. Elevators were invented in 1857. They made taller buildings possible.

Long before skyscrapers, people built towers. Towers were usually made out of stone. They were dark inside because there were no windows. A hole for a window might weaken the walls. Then the walls might fall down. For a long time, buildings were not very tall. Then **cathedral** builders figured out a way to strengthen tall buildings. The builders made long arms out of stone. These arms, called **buttresses**, supported the weight of the walls. The arms made it possible for huge stone cathedrals to have big windows.

Can you imagine buttresses holding up a stone skyscraper? The buttresses would have to be huge! For skyscrapers, a different kind of building material was needed. That's where Henry Bessemer came in.

Meet Henry Bessemer

Sir Henry Bessemer was born in Great Britain in 1813. He invented paint with "gold" powder. He made paint look like gold using bits of brass. His paint was popular and made him rich. Then he studied ways to make steel. He came up with the Bessemer process. The process was based on a centuries-old method used by Chinese metalworkers. The workers blew air through iron, making steel. Bessemer wanted to make stronger steel for cannons. The cannons of the time were not strong enough for powerful shells. Bessemer had many other interests, too. For instance, he made an official seal for the British government. The seal could not be copied. He was knighted in 1879 for his work.

William Kelly tried blowing air through melted pig iron. That is iron in its rough form. Blowing air though the metal removed substances that weakened the metal.

He sold his idea to me. I remember my excitement the first time I tried to improve on his idea.

The furnace man thought I'd end up with heavy melted metal. What I got was something much better.

I created my own kind of steel.

Strongest Shapes

paper and pencil

two equal piles
of books

pieces of
heavy paper

masking tape

weights, such as bits of clay or
broken crayons of equal sizes

---

1 Use the paper and tape to make beams about 18 inches (½ meter) long. Try different shapes, such as a cylinder, a square tube, or a triangular tube.

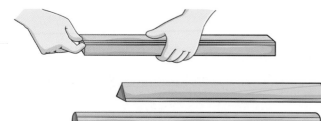

2 Arrange the books into two piles. Leave a gap between them that the piece of paper can reach across.

---

3 First bridge the gap with a flat piece of paper. Put weights on the paper. What happens?

4 Next bridge the gap with the beams. Test each beam by adding weights a few at a time. Record the number of weights each beam holds. Which shape beam would you want in a building?

WHO WOULD HAVE THOUGHT?

Making Skyscrapers

George A. Fuller made tall buildings safer. His first tall building, the Tacoma Building, was finished in 1889. Fuller used beams made of Bessemer steel to create "cages" within the walls. These cages help support the weight of the building. They share the weight of the load. After Fuller's death, his son ran his company. That company built one of New York City's first skyscrapers, the Flatiron Building. The triangular building was completed in 1902. Many other skyscrapers followed. The tallest building in the United States today is the Sears Tower. It opened in 1973. Its height at roof level is 1,451 feet (442 m). That is more than the length of four football fields in a row. Talk about scraping the sky!

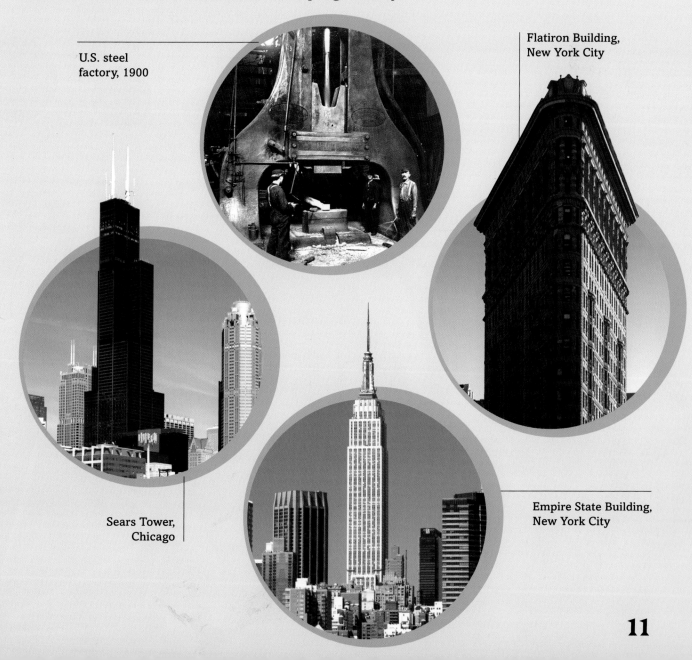

U.S. steel factory, 1900

Flatiron Building, New York City

Sears Tower, Chicago

Empire State Building, New York City

Spaceship Earth

Richard Buckminster Fuller was a famous thinker. He is known, in part, for his work with geodesic domes. A dome is a curved structure, like an upside-down bowl. A geodesic dome has a surface made of lightweight, straight shapes. The shapes form a grid of triangles. These triangles are held in tension against one another. One triangle supports another. They make the dome a very strong structure.

Fuller was fascinated by geodesic domes. He believed the domes could shelter many people, yet be made with inexpensive materials. Fuller thought the domes could solve many housing problems. He studied beehives and other items with grids to support his ideas.

Meet Buckminster Fuller

R. Buckminster Fuller was born in Milton, Massachusetts, in 1895. He was self-educated. He was the first man in his family who did not graduate from Harvard University. Fuller had an original mind. At one point, he stopped talking. He lived almost two years without speaking. Why? He didn't want to say anything untrue.

Fuller wanted to help humanity. He looked for ways to solve problems. He looked at housing and energy. He also looked at food supply, pollution, and transportation. Fuller earned more than two thousand **patents**. He wrote twenty-five books. He gave a series of famous talks in 1975 called "Everything I Know." These talks lasted forty-two hours! He spoke about architecture, math, and more.

I look for building materials that are strong and lightweight. It is important for everyone on Earth to have a place to live.

If you pack triangles of material together, a surface is created that is both strong and lightweight.

Shapes fascinated me. I actually made a map of Earth with eight triangles and six rectangles.

I believe in an idea I call Spaceship Earth. Our creative abilities are unlimited. We can use our abilities and technology to create a better future for the planet.

Fallen Arches

telephone books or
other thick books

4 raw eggs

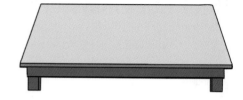

table

Scotch tape

sharp knife

adult helper

1 Carefully punch a hole in the small end of each egg. Pour out the insides. You can save the insides for a recipe.

2 Wrap tape around the middle of each eggshell, like a belt. Ask an adult to help you cut each eggshell in half, along the tape.

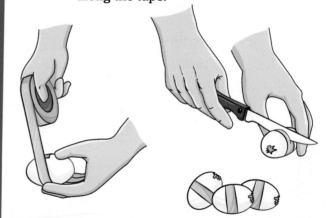

3 You end up with eight eggshell "domes." Place four domes of the same size on the table. Arrange them in a rectangle. They will work like arches.

4 One by one, place books on the shells. How many books can you place on top before the shells break? It is amazing how strong a simple shape can be.

WHO WOULD HAVE THOUGHT?

Life in a Dome

Buckminster Fuller's ideas live on. Spaceship Earth is now the name of a famous geodesic dome. It is featured at Disney's EPCOT Center. Geodesic domes show up in sports and entertainment centers across the world. Architects use them to build houses, garages, and greenhouses. The dome shape continues to fascinate people. **Waterproofing** domes can be a problem, though. This is why there are few dome-shaped homes.

Fuller had a plan to place a dome high over New York City. The dome would keep out pollution. Weather would be controlled inside. The environment would be carefully watched. Is it possible that we will live in a world as he imagined?

EPCOT Center, Florida

Science World, Vancouver, Canada

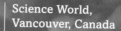

Building Bridges

A log can be used as a simple bridge for a small creek. You need something more to bridge longer distances. The Golden Gate Bridge in San Francisco covers a long distance across a bay. It is a **suspension bridge**. Suspension bridges can run across distances greater than a mile (1½ km).

On a suspension bridge, the roadway hangs from cables. Towers are drilled into rock or concrete blocks. Cables string from one tower to another. Smaller cables hang from the main cables and hold the roadway.

Long ago, cables on small suspension bridges were made of rope or even plant vines. Modern suspension bridges needed stronger materials, however. That's why John Roebling invented a wire rope. It revolutionized bridge building.

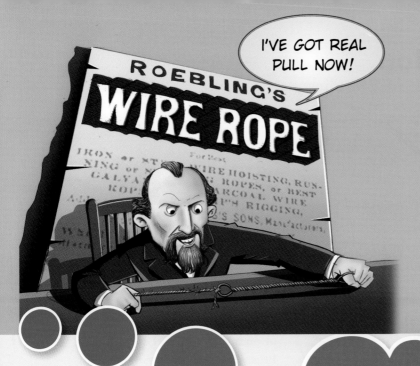

I'VE GOT REAL PULL NOW!

ROEBLING'S WIRE ROPE

Meet John Roebling

John Roebling moved to the United States in 1831. He was born in 1806 in Prussia, now called Germany. He settled near Pittsburgh and worked as an **engineer**. His projects included improving canals. In some places, the canals were too narrow for big **barges**. The barges had to be towed on railways across land. The towropes were made of a plant material called hemp. These ropes were thick and hard to handle. They had to be replaced often. Roebling read that German engineers were making rope out of wire. He decided to make a wire rope, too. He made a strong wire rope that was perfect for suspension bridges.

My bosses didn't think my rope idea would work. Then they saw the finished product. They knew I was right.

I used the wire rope to build my first suspension bridge in 1847.

The best was yet to come.

I built a bridge across the Niagara River near Niagara Falls. People called it a wonder of the world.

Suspension in Action

two hardcover books
of the same size

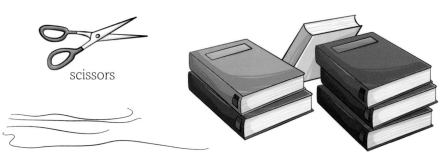

scissors

several feet or
meters of string

four to six
heavy books

 1 Tie a loop of string around each of the same-sized books. Tie a third string to the loops. Stand the two books on end, making the third string hang between them.

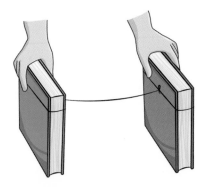

2 Set the books upright on a table or on a floor without carpeting. Press down on the string hanging between the books. What happens?

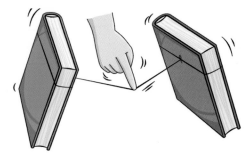

 3 Stand the same books about 10 inches (25 cm) apart. Remove the string. Drape a longer string over the books. Leave string hanging at both ends.

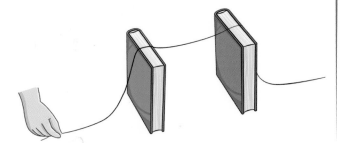

4 Stack heavy books on each end of string. Press again on the center of the string. What happens?

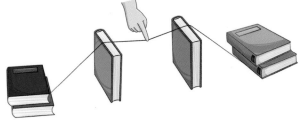

WHO WOULD HAVE THOUGHT?

Going, Going, Gone

Suspension bridges need to be able to move a bit when there is weight on them. You don't want the bridge to move too much, however! Consider the Tacoma Narrows Bridge. When it opened in 1940, the bridge was the third longest suspension bridge in the world. It earned fame because of its behavior in wind. People noticed that the bridge went from side to side. It also went up and down. Drivers watched as vehicles in front of them disappeared and reappeared as the bridge moved. Four months after it opened, it fell. The bridge was rebuilt as a pair of bridges. They reopened in 1949. Now, all bridges must be tested for their strength against wind.

Akashi–Kaikyo Bridge, Japan

Golden Gate Bridge, U.S.A.

Humber Bridge, Great Britain

Verrazano Narrows Bridge, U.S.A.

Underwater Connection

The English Channel is the waterway between France and England. The Channel Tunnel connects England and France beneath that water. The tunnel is actually three tunnels. Trains run in two of them. The third tunnel is for service vehicles, which keep the tunnels in good repair. Passengers can drive onto the train in cars or buses!

Having a Channel Tunnel was a dream for many years. In 1802, Albert Mathieu-Favier, a French engineer, offered the first plan. Horse-drawn vehicles would move through a tunnel between France and England. There would be an island in the middle. On the island, the horses could be switched with another team. Oil lamps would light the tunnel. Chimneys would clear the air.

Favier's plan never came to be. Many other plans were started and stopped before today's tunnel was built. Engineers such as Fred Beaumont had to figure out how to get the digging done.

Meet Colonel Fred Beaumont

How do you cut through rock safely? What do you do with the leftover pieces? How do you power the parts of the machine? Colonel Fred Beaumont invented a machine that could spin and cut through rock. It could leave the waste behind. It could press air to use as a form of power. Though modern machines are better, his machine was the first.

Frederick Edward Blackett Beaumont was born in England in 1833. He served in many wars. Beaumont was working for a railroad when he perfected his ideas for the tunnel-boring machine.

I became interested in tunnel digging after serving in the military.

We looked for a way to dig tunnels without dangerous explosives. We didn't want to put people in danger.

I made a tunneling machine. It worked pretty well.

Thomas English built the machine used to test the difficulty of digging through the channel. Somehow, I got credit for that. History can play tricks on us!

Water Pressure

hammer
and nail

yardstick or
meterstick

milk carton

pitcher

paper and
pencil

1 Using the hammer and nail, make holes 1 inch (2.5 cm) apart on one side of the carton. Make holes the same size, going up and down a straight line.

2 Stand the carton on a surface that won't be damaged by water. Place the measuring stick so that the carton's holes point toward it.

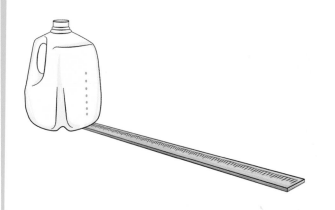

3 Fill the pitcher with water. Pour that water into the carton with the holes. Water will squirt out.

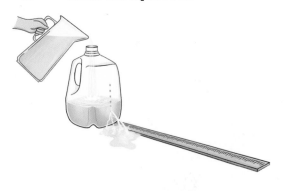

4 Measure the distance the water squirts from each hole. Keep track of your findings with the paper and pencil. The deeper the water, the higher the pressure!

WHO WOULD HAVE THOUGHT?
A Long Time in the Making

In 1904 France and England began work on a tunnel across the channel. The countries had disagreements, however. It wasn't until 1986 that they signed a tunnel treaty. The governments then hired EuroTunnel to build and operate a tunnel between the countries. The company's fifty-five-year contract began in 1987. Construction started on both sides of the channel. The project did not go smoothly. There were concerns about plants and animals. There were delays and extra costs. Everything seemed to cause problems. The Channel Tunnel was finished in 1994. Think of all it went through from an idea to reality!

illustration of early work on the tunnel

tunnel shuttle terminal

modern tunnel

Floating Cargo

Container ships carry most of the dry **cargo** in the world. These ships carry huge containers. Their long, boxy containers are super strong. They can hold tremendous weight even when stacked.

The first containers like them were used to move cargo on the rails. In the early 1900s, railways loaded big containers onto flatcars. Later on, the containers were carried by trucks. During World War II, the military put the container trucks on board ships that could carry them across the seas. The trucks added extra weight, however. Malcom McLean fixed the problem. He built special containers. The containers could be lifted off the back of trucks. The same containers could be put onto ships. McLean's containers were not opened after being filled. That kept the cargo safe from theft and damage. Not loading and unloading the contents saved time and money, too.

The first ship carrying McLean's containers sailed from Newark, New Jersey, to Houston, Texas in 1956. Soon, these floating superstructures filled ocean ports.

EASY DOES IT!

Meet Malcolm McLean

Malcom McLean is also known for inventing a way to lift patients out of hospital beds. This inventor was born in North Carolina in 1913. During the 1930s, he worked as a truck driver. McLean hauled goods for farmers. He often had to wait while crates were taken from his truck and loaded onto ships.

McLean then built a trucking company. With his profits, he made containers that could be separated from trucks. The steel containers protected their contents. The containers could be stacked to save space. The new method cut costs by more than thirty times. McLean is among those who have changed history by changing construction.

The military was driving trucks onto ships in order to move cargo.

I could see this situation could be improved. Too much space was being wasted.

I thought that we should have standard sizes for containers.

Not everyone supported my idea. One official remarked that he'd like to sink it!

Carrying Cargo

pennies

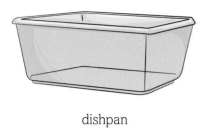

dishpan

aluminum foil

measuring cup

1 Use the aluminum foil to make three different shapes of boats. One should be flat with short sides, like a barge.

2 Use the measuring cup to pour water into each boat. Make sure each boat holds the same amount of water.

3 Empty the boats. Fill the dishpan halfway with water. Place the first boat in the water. Add pennies to the boat, one at a time, until the boat sinks.

4 Dry the pennies. Repeat the experiment with each boat. Count the pennies to see which kind of boat holds the most weight.

WHO WOULD HAVE THOUGHT?

Supertankers

Imagine a building that is a quarter mile (½ km) tall. It is as wide as half a football field. Now turn that building on its side and float it in the ocean. Some supertankers are actually that size. Crew members use bicycles to get around on these big ships. Even without cargo, these supertankers can weigh hundreds of thousands of tons (tonnes). Their fuel storage tanks are enormous, too. One fuel storage tank can be as big as a large church.

Supertankers can be too big to enter a port. Why build such big ships? Large sizes and small crews make the biggest profits. Engineers continue to make improvements to these ships. Today's supertankers are bigger, faster, and safer than ever before.

Timeline

AROUND 2630 B.C.
Imhotep builds the first
step pyramid.

220–200 B.C.
The most famous part of the
Great Wall of China is built.

226
The ancient Romans
finish the last of
their aqueducts.

1802
Albert Mathieu-Favier
proposes an idea for
a tunnel under the
English Channel.

1841
John Roebling invents
a new kind of wire.

1856
The Bessemer
process for making
steel is discovered.

1857
The elevator
is installed.

1987
Tunnel construction begins on both sides of the English Channel.

1973
The Sears Tower opens.

1956
Malcom McLean sends off the first modern container ship.

1954
R. Buckminster Fuller patents his geodesic dome.

1940
The Tacoma Narrows Bridge opens—and collapses.

1874
Colonel Fred Beaumont invents his tunnel-boring machine.

1889
The first skyscraper is built.

Glossary

aqueduct large pipe that carries water over a long distance; also, a structure like a bridge used to support the pipe.

architect someone who designs buildings and oversees their construction.

barge a large boat, which often has a flat bottom, built for carrying heavy freight.

buttress a strong support built against a structure to hold it up or make it stronger.

cargo the goods carried by a ship, a truck, an airplane, or another vehicle.

cathedral a large and important church.

engineer a person trained to plan and design structures like bridges, roads, and tunnels.

fulcrum the support, or point of rest, on which a lever turns when moving a load.

lever a bar that turns at one of its points, used to move a load placed at a second point by force applied at a third.

mastaba a structure with a flat roof and sloping sides, built over a place of burial.

patent a document granting the rights to an invention.

skyscraper a tall building with many floors, or stories.

suspension bridge a bridge that hangs from cables that are anchored by towers.

technology the use of science for practical purposes, as in the fields of engineering and industry.

waterproofing sealing something to keep out water.

To Learn More

Books

Bridges: Amazing Structures to Design, Build & Test by Carol A. Johmann. Williamson Publishing Company, 1999.

Skyscrapers: Uncovering Technology by Chris Oxlade. Firefly Books, 2006.

Super Structures by Phil Wilkinson. DK Children's Books, 2008.

Websites

This Buckminster Fuller Institute site looks at Fuller's many innovative ideas, including his work with geodesic domes.
http://www.bfi.org/

Building Big is a PBS site that gives the inside story on bridges, domes, skyscrapers, dams, and tunnels.
http://www.pbs.org/wgbh/buildingbig/

Pyramid, by PBS, provides an online excavation that unlocks some of the secrets behind the amazing pyramids.
http://www.pbs.org/wgbh/nova/pyramid/

Index